This Bramcost Publications edition is an unabridged republication
of the rare original work first published in 1929.

www.BramcostPublications.com

ISBN 10: 1-934268-98-4
ISBN 13: 978-1-934268-98-8

Library of Congress Control Number: 2009923964

**Bramcost
Publications**

THE SEW-IT BOOK

By

RACHEL TAFT DIXON

Author, with Marjorie Hartwell,
of "The Make-It Book"

Illustrated by

MARJORIE HARTWELL *and* RACHEL TAFT DIXON

THE CONTENTS

THE INTRODUCTION

This introduction is for GROWN-UPS.   The book really begins on Page 7.

There is no greater mistake grown-ups can make than to think children are like themselves.   Yet most of us make that mistake—we think if we like a thing, we have only to simplify it a bit and make it easier and it will be just right for a child.   So when we see clever and ingenious toys we are sure that their very completeness is the measure of their worth to the child.   We say: "No little girl can fail to be charmed with this lovely wardrobe for her doll!   See the frocks and underwear—tiny, perfect copies of real French designs. And all ready to be put on her doll, even to the hooks and snaps!"

Now, the truth of the matter is that children most want, not complete and finished playthings, but a chance to take materials and turn them into products themselves.   Instead of a finished outfit for her doll, a little girl most wants to take part in producing one.

Perhaps we may get the child's point of view if we try to remember the things that gave us the most pleasure when we were children.   Was there anything dearer than a rag doll?   Wasn't it taken to bed at night and to breakfast the next morning?   Wouldn't it have been fun when you were a few years older to have been able to make a rag doll?   And the pride a girl feels in making cushions and curtains for a room that is really her own! Does furnishing an entire house when one is grown up equal it?

The most successful gift I ever saw a child receive came to a little girl on her eleventh birthday.   It was a roll of textiles—about a dozen pieces, mostly half-yard lengths, of brilliant hued silks and gay prints.   Her first delight was in handling them and draping them on furniture; then, when she had become acquainted with them, she began to plan what she could make of them.

Miss Dixon in THE SEW-IT BOOK offers guidance for such a situation.   Many of the charming projects she suggests, however, may be carried out without purchase of special materials.   Her directions are simple and direct and will enable a child to produce satisfying results.

Sound educational values are incorporated in this, as in the other volumes of THE RAND McNALLY ACTIVITIES BOOKS, of which series THE SEW-IT BOOK is a part.   These books give boys and girls an opportunity to use their constructive powers to create things they need in carrying out various purposes.

In addition, THE SEW-IT BOOK provides training needed in adult life.   While it may be true that present-day skill in manufacture makes it unnecessary for most women to be producers of clothing, they are all consumers and purchasers.   Experience in childhood such as Miss Dixon makes possible through THE SEW-IT BOOK is excellent preparation for intelligent purchase and use of clothing.

That she has been able to incorporate such permanent values in activities so full of pleasure and interest is extremely fortunate.

MIRIAM BLANTON HUBER

TEACHERS COLLEGE
COLUMBIA UNIVERSITY

THE SEW-IT BOOK

THE SEWING BOX

THIS is your own sewing book. It will show you how to make pretty things not only for your doll family, but for yourself and for your room. There will be directions for sewing things that make attractive and very welcome gifts, too.

Perhaps you know how to baste, how to make running stitches, backstitches, and buttonhole stitches, but if you need them, there are charts to remind you about these and other useful stitches.

First of all you must have a place to keep your sewing materials—a sewing box with places for scissors, tape measure, thimble, needles and pins, thread, and bias-folded tape. Besides these things, a pincushion and needlebook are both necessary for your sewing box. A pencil and small notebook will be useful, too. Ask Mother if you may have a paper of pins, a paper of crewel needles for heavy embroidery cotton and yarn, and a paper of long-eyed needles—5 to 10 size is the best for your work. A small tape needle will be necessary for running in draw strings and elastic. A spool of No. 40 white thread, one of 70, and some colored embroidery floss or yarn will be all the thread you need to begin work.

Be sure your scissors are sharp. Have an emery tucked in your sewing box for keeping your needle bright so it will slip through material easily. Clean hands are pretty important, so be sure to wash them before starting to sew.

When you sit down to sew have a clear space on a table before you, where you can lay your material to cut and baste. The old saying "A good workman is known by his tools" is very true, and it is quite as true that a good workman makes the conditions under which he works just as favorable as possible. You can do this also. Sit in a comfortable chair and give yourself plenty of room on the table to lay out your work. Have a scrap basket near by for the snips and threads.

If you carry out all these suggestions you will find they will help you to enjoy sewing.

A BAG FOR MARBLES OR BUTTONS

Materials: Monks cloth (or burlap) 7 inches by 17 inches, embroidery cotton or yarn, 1 yard of colored tape

This bag will be useful for your sewing box, or for a gift. Of course it may be made of almost any material, but this bag is of monks cloth or burlap because these materials are so easy to decorate with running stitches and cross-stitch. Any material in a coarse basket weave is just as good.

If your material is larger than the size needed, measure off a piece 7 inches wide and 17 inches long, and place pins to mark the length and width. Find the thread nearest the pin, then cut along the thread to make a perfectly straight edge. This is called cutting by the thread. On finer materials it is usually necessary to draw out the thread so that the line will be easier to follow.

Overcast the raw edges so they will not ravel while you are working. It is easier to put the decorative stitches on the material before sewing the sides of the bag. Consult the opposite page for ideas of decorative stitches for your bag. Several suggestions are given for combinations of these borders. You will find that a simple combination is best, using plain running stitches, running stitches with a slight change, and one row of a quite different pattern of stitch. The threads of the cloth are

divided off into little squares by the weave. Decide how long your stitch should be to look well. It will not be practical to make any stitches longer than $\frac{1}{2}$ inch, for the longer the stitch, the more easily it catches on things and pulls out of shape. Start the stitching border 2 inches from one end of the material for a top border. Figure 1 has a border $1\frac{3}{4}$ inches wide.

The initial is done in cross-stitch in the center of the side, after the border is finished. Of course you may like to make two or three initials instead, and you may wish to work the border on both sides of the bag instead of on just one side. You may choose the pattern for your border, the placing of the border, and the color scheme. For a border at the bottom of the bag, measure about $\frac{1}{2}$ inch from the middle of the strip of material.

Monks cloth usually comes in a grayish tone which makes a good background for many colors. Mother's box of left-over bits of yarn may provide wools for embroidering. Heather-mixture yarn is very attractive when combined with one or two rows of gay-colored yarn. Embroidery cotton should be heavy, or else three-ply. Use a large crewel needle with a big eye so there will be no trouble in threading it, and be sure to carry your borders straight across by the thread of the cloth.

When the border and the initial (if you use one) are done, fold the strip of material wrong side out with the ends together, and sew up the sides from the fold to a point 2 inches from the ends, making a $\frac{3}{8}$-inch seam.

Now hem down the seam allowance for the 2 inches left open so the edges will not interfere with the draw strings. Next, fold the hem at the top to form a casing for the draw strings. This should use the 2-inch allowance at the top. Pin in place, run a basting around, then hem down quite closely.

For the draw strings, cut the yard of tape in half and thread one of the pieces on a tape needle. Starting at one side of the bag, run the tape around through the casing, bringing the needle out at the starting point. Knot the two ends of the piece of tape together. Run the other piece of tape around through the casing in the same way, from the opposite side of the bag, and knot the ends together.

That was not a hard piece of sewing, was it? Now that you have made this you will know how to make bags for other uses. One might be cut large and long for a laundry bag, another might be cut in a large square with the casing top sewed over oval or round embroidery hoops to carry it by. The sides should be left open for three inches below the casing. This makes a splendid knitting bag. The hoops may be wound tightly with ribbon or you may prefer to cover them with shirred ribbon. Such a bag is better made of cretonne or other material that does not need decoration.

The stitches you have used for decorating the marble bag will be useful for clothes as well as for bags. Yarn embroidery of the simplest sort makes a perfect decoration for a jersey frock. On this page, among the decorative stitches, there are some designs which may be worked easily on any sort of material when you have learned to make stitches of even length, in a straight line.

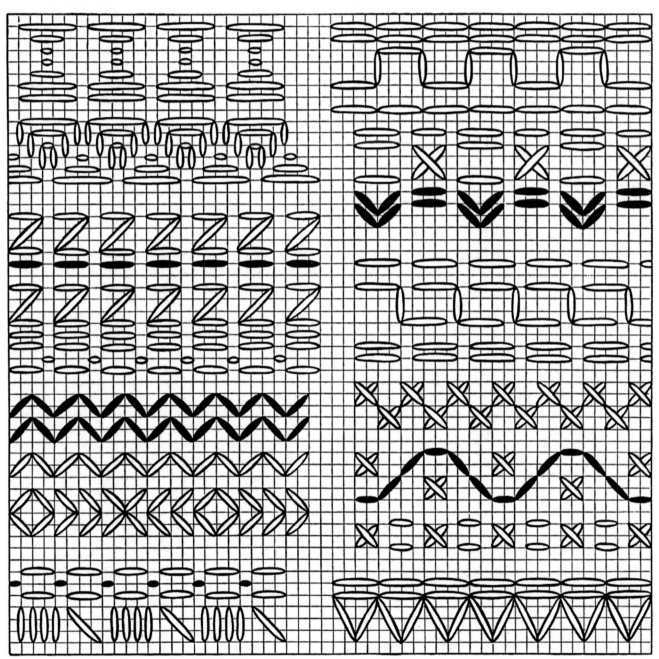

A TOWEL

Materials: One yard of toweling, heavy single-strand embroidery cotton, cross-stitch canvas

If everyone had such pretty towels as you can make, they would find dish wiping more fun. It takes just a yard of toweling for one towel. Linen toweling is better than cotton because linen absorbs moisture more quickly. Kitchen toweling may be bought with crossbars of red or of dark blue, and it is this sort that makes the gayest towels. Get

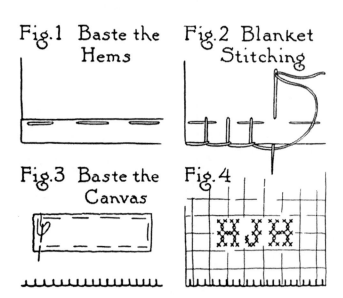

embroidery cotton matching the color of the crossbars to use for the cross-stitch monogram and the blanket stitching on the hems.

In making the towels, first even the ends by pulling a thread and trimming off on this line. Then fold a hem about ¼ inch deep across each end and baste it (Fig. 1). Blanket stitching is done on the right side of the towel. Use a needle with a large eye so there will be no trouble in threading it. The stitches should be far enough from the edge to reach just beyond the hem (about ¼ inch) and the space between the blanket stitches should be the same distance. See Figure 2 for a diagram of blanket stitching. When the hems are finished, fold the towel double lengthwise and crease the fold at one end to mark the middle.

Consult the cross-stitch alphabet on page 11 for the letters you will use. A single initial is good for marking the towel, or you may like to use the whole

monogram of two or three letters, as in the illustration. Count the number of squares in each letter, and allow two squares between the letters, to find just how large a piece of canvas you are going to need.

Cut the canvas, and baste it 1 inch above the hem at the middle of the towel (Fig. 4). If there are to be three letters, work the middle initial first so it will be centered exactly. When the cross-stitching is finished, the canvas threads are unraveled and pulled out (Fig. 5).

Another way to mark the towel is to place the cross-stitch letters down in the left-hand corner of the towel about 1 inch from the side of the towel and 1 inch from the hem.

A CROSS-STITCH BIB FOR BABY

Materials: A piece of linen 12 inches by 16 inches, three-strand embroidery cotton, ½-inch white cotton tape, cross-stitch canvas

Babies often object to having bibs tied on, but if they had bibs with such cunning little cross-stitch creatures to watch, they would forget the strings. The brighter the color the more quickly will the baby's eye be attracted. That is why bright red is such a good color for the cross-stitching.

If you buy ½ yard of cross-stitch canvas you will have enough to do the cross-stitched articles in this book which require canvas. It may be bought in fine and coarse qualities, but for your work, canvas taking about eight cross-stitches to an inch is best.

The pattern of the bib is cut first. Measure off on a sheet of paper a piece 16 inches long and 6 inches wide, as in the diagram. To draw the neck line, mark off from one corner 3 inches on the short side and 3½ inches on the long side. Connect these two points with a curved line, as in the diagram. Cut out this curve and around the straight sides and you have the pattern of one side of the bib.

Now take your linen and even the edges very carefully by pulling a thread and cutting on the line. Trim it to the length of the bib pattern and to twice the width of the pattern. Fold the linen lengthwise with the edges exactly together, and lay the pattern on the linen with the long side and neck opening against the folded edge (see diagram). Pin in place and cut out the curving line for the neck.

Finishing the edges of the bib comes next. Fold a narrow hem—about ¼ inch deep—down the long

sides of the bib, and baste. Next turn up a hem ¾ inch wide across the bottom of the bib, and baste carefully. Fold narrow hems across the top ends and baste.

Basting may seem like a waste of time, but it really is not, for each basting stitch is a good helper, holding your hem in place as you sew.

Now hem all the basted hems. This is good straight-ahead work that gives you a chance to see what even little stitches you can make. It is best to overhand the ends of the bottom hem.

The neck binding of soft tape ends in strings for tying. Lay the bib right side up on a flat surface and begin pinning the tape around the neck curve ¼ inch from the edge, leaving an 8-inch end hanging for a tie string at each end of the curve. Take care not to stretch the curved edge as you work, or the bib will not fit smoothly. Now baste the edge of the tape in an even curve and sew with neat little running stitches close to the edge. Fold the tape

over so it will cover the raw edge of the material and meet the line of stitches on the under side. Baste the tape binding in place carefully, then hem the edge down.

The last part of making the bib is the best. Crease the bib down the middle, then crease it across 2½ inches from the bottom edge. This marks the middle of the bib, and the bottom line of the spot of cross-stitch embroidery.

You have a choice of animals to decorate the bib (page 11). Decide which one of the designs you prefer, then count how many cross-stitches high it is and how many cross-stitches wide. Be sure to see that your piece of canvas is big enough for the design. You will find the blue threads in the canvas mark off five squares. Baste the canvas on at the horizontal crease, with the middle of the canvas over the center crease. Begin your cross-stitches at the middle of the pattern, for you will find that is the easiest way to place the design exactly in the center.

The embroidery is in one color. Red or blue makes a good choice. First cross-stitch the dish,

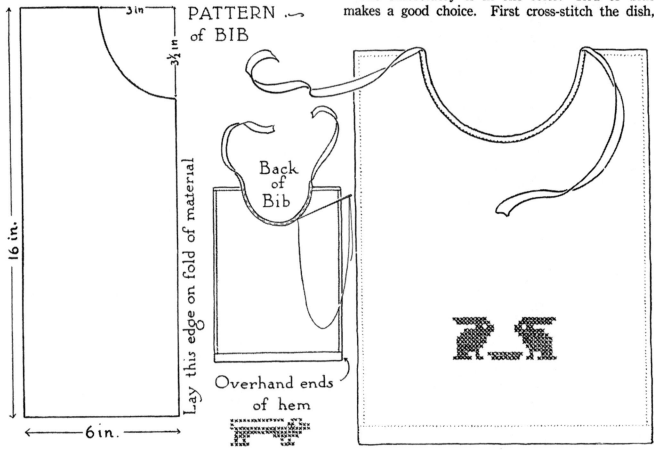

PATTERN of BIB

16 in.

6 in.

3 in

3½ in

Lay this edge on fold of material

Back of Bib

Overhand ends of hem

then begin to cross-stitch the feet of the figure on one side. Make all your cross-stitches cross in the same direction.

If you wish, Baby's initials may be worked higher up. The simple alphabet will help you. Work the middle initial first, then space the others at least two squares apart.

Isn't it a jolly bib? And won't Baby crow when he sees it? Perhaps when he will not eat as much as he should, a story about his bib animals will amuse him while he swallows the extra spoonfuls.

A BUTTON-BOY BIB

Materials: Linen, ½-inch cotton tape, ¼-inch linen tape, ⅛-inch linen tape, ⅜-inch pearl buttons, ¼-inch pearl buttons, a bit of colored linen or gingham, cotton embroidery floss in same color

Have you ever tried drawing funny little figures with a small circle for head and straight lines for arms, legs and body? They are sometimes called match-stick figures. It is great fun to see how lively you can make them appear. They can dance, jump, skate, and do many other things.

These Button Boys are done in the same fashion. Of course you will want to make your own Button Boys. To look well on a bib, they should not be taller than 2¼ inches. Draw two parallel lines 2¼ inches apart, then draw several pairs of match-stick figures between these lines as the diagram suggests. When you have decided which drawing you like best, cut it out on the parallel lines. Hold the paper up against the window with the drawing next the window glass, and trace the figures on the other side of the paper.

Now proceed to make the bib, following the directions for the cross-stitch bib, creasing down the middle and creasing again crosswise in order to place the decoration evenly.

Trim off a little colored linen patch even by the thread, measuring your design and making the patch of the same width and length, with a ⅜-inch seam allowed on all sides. Fold under ⅜ inch and baste down. Crease the patch across the middle the narrow way of the piece. Lay the patch right side up on the bib with center creases together and the lower edge of the patch at the horizontal crease on the bib. Pin in place, then baste. This is blanket-stitched onto the bib with the colored embroidery cotton. Make the stitches of an even size, about ³⁄₁₆ inch long and the same distance apart. When this is done lay your sketch of the two Button Boys on the colored patch, with the underside tracing next the material, and the parallel edges of the paper even with the edges of the patch. Pin in place. Rub over the figures firmly with a spool. This transfers enough for you to follow the design, though you may wish to trace the lines with a fine pointed pencil to make them clearer.

The ⅛-inch tapes are basted on first, keeping the outline under the middle of the tape. One strip of tape forms both arms, another strip, by folding over in the middle, makes the legs. Bent knees and elbows are done by folding the tape over. Turn in the ends of the tape at hands and feet, and sew the tape on both edges with fine white thread in running stitch. Sew one side first, then the other. Use the wider linen tape for the body, turning under both ends of the tape, basting, and sewing with running stitch.

Last of all, the buttons are sewed on with the colored embroidery cotton. The face seems to have more expression if the button has four holes sewed in crossed stitches. Of course a button of the larger size makes the face. It does not matter if the smaller buttons have only two holes. Before sewing them on, experiment by placing the buttons in different positions to see how they look best. Sometimes

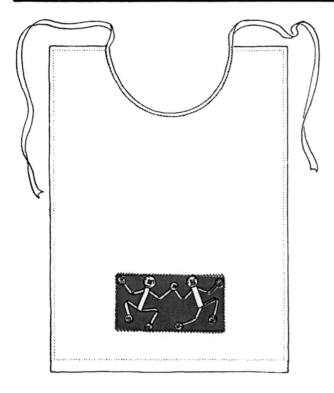

A RAFFIA EMBROIDERED PURSE

Materials: Cross-stitch canvas 6¾ inches by 10¼ inches, raffia, blunt-pointed needle No. 18, silk for lining

If you have never sewed with raffia you will be surprised to find how quickly your work progresses. Raffia may be bought in a number of colors besides the natural color. Of course you can dye it if you wish, but if you do, be careful to make the color fast so it cannot come off on the hands or gloves. Dyes for cotton and linen are the sort to use.

The raffia is worked on a foundation of cross-stitch canvas which should have about twelve squares to the inch, to work out correctly with the designs illustrated. If your purse turns out to be a bit smaller or larger, it will not matter. If you make a purse for Mother, it should be about twice the size of your own. These designs are 63 squares wide and about 95 squares long, except Figure 4 which is 64 squares wide. The canvas on which they are worked has twelve squares to an inch and measures 6¾ inches by 10¼ inches. This allows ¾ inch to turn under on all sides.

The designs are suggested by patterns made by American Indians. Some of these were woven in cloth and others in beads. The diagram shows the stitches used for the raffia work. You see they are few and not hard to do. It is possible to use many

placing the head on one side makes the figure more amusing. If you wish the figures to have roller skates, instead of one button for a foot, sew on two buttons for each skate as in the illustration.

Don't you think any baby should be proud of such a bib?

It would be fun to make a little colored linen or gingham button bag trimmed with a Button Boy dancing on the outside. To make the bag, follow the directions for cutting the bag for marbles, then sew the Button Boy in place on one side of the bag. Follow the same directions for making the bag, and run in draw strings of linen tape. This would make a gay little Christmas gift, if carried out in brilliant colored material.

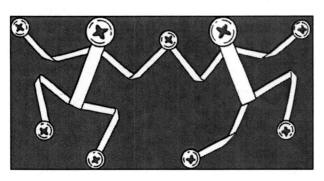

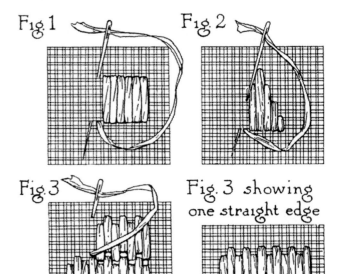

Fig 1

Fig 2

Fig 3

Fig. 3 showing one straight edge

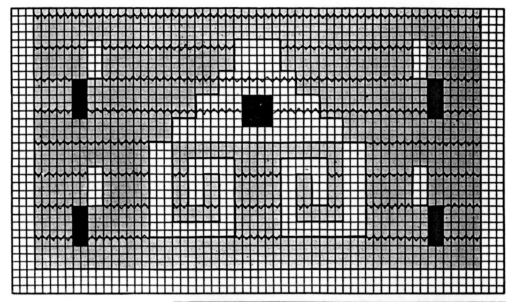

Fig. 4

SOUTH
AMERICAN
INDIAN
DESIGNS

Fig. 5

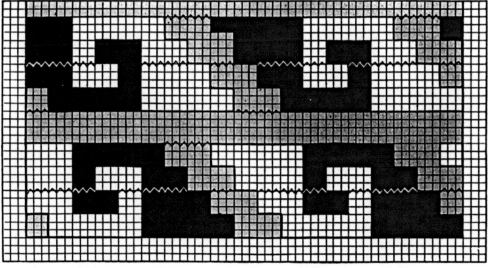

other stitches such as are used in embroidering with cotton and wool, but until you are used to sewing with raffia, which is stiffer, it is well to try easier ways of working with it.

Figure 1 shows an over-and-over stitch used to fill in patterns and borders with square outlines, such as the spots of design on Figures 4 and 5. Figure 2 shows the way to fill slanting edged units of design, such as the body and feet of the bird design in Figure 7.

Since the designs are worked by the thread of the canvas it is not necessary to draw the lines of the design except for the slanting lines. For these it is a great help to have a fine, sharp, ruled line to follow. Find where this line should begin and end, then draw the line between these points.

Figure 3 shows the background stitch used for Figures 4 and 7. The bands of design in Figure 6 are done in this stitch. The fine sawtooth line on the designs shows where this stitch is used. The borders are all worked as in Figure 1. The corners are turned by working to the slanting line connecting the inside and outside corner of the border. Where the background meets the design or the border, the sewing is on a straight line, of course.

To help you in selecting and arranging the colors of each design these suggestions are given:

Figure 4 calls for three colors or shades of raffia. Use natural raffia for the border and the light units. Use tan raffia for the background, and make the little black spots either black or a dark brown.

If you wear navy blue more than brown you will prefer to use a navy-blue background, with the tiny spots embroidered in cherry red. The natural-color

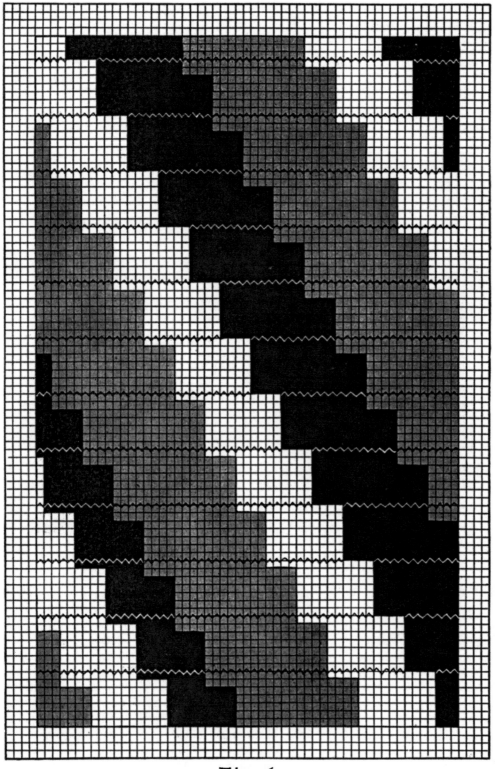

Fig. 6

raffia will be right for the border and light parts of the design.

Figure 5 needs three colors for the three shades illustrated: natural color for the white, yellow for the gray, and orange for the black part.

Figure 6 requires three shades. Natural color, beige, and henna will be suitable for this design. Natural color forms the border and the white zig-zag portions of the design, henna is used on the black portions, and beige on the other parts.

Another combination is natural color with light green and dark green. The design is one that suggests shaded effects. If you made a grown-up's purse, it would be effective embroidered

NORTH AMERICAN INDIAN DESIGN

Fig. 7

NORTH
AMERICAN
INDIAN
DESIGN

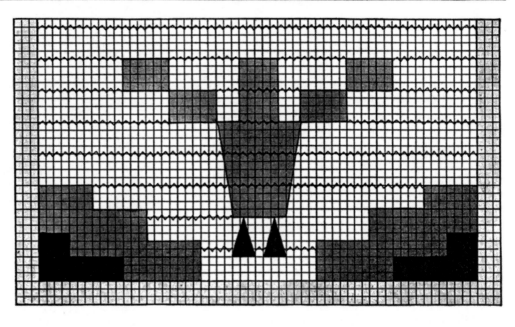

in natural color, gray,
and black. Bright
colors are prettier for
you. What they are
to be depends a little
on what color of hat
you are likely to wear when carrying the purse.

Figure 7 is embroidered in four different colors:
natural for the background, henna for the bird and
the corners, and black for the little corner spots
and the bird's feet. The border is worked in beige
raffia.

Figure 6 is the only design that has a pattern
worked on the whole purse. The other designs have
a plain raffia background and the narrow border is
continued around the sides.

If the raffia is stiff, it is a good plan to pull each
needleful through a damp cloth before sewing.

Before starting to work the designs shown in
Figure 5 or Figure 7 it is best to crease your canvas
through the middle, lengthwise, so that the center
of the design may be placed evenly. By count-
ing squares on your canvas you can place all
the units the right distance apart. Keep your
canvas flat, and take care not to pull your stitches
too tight. Squeeze them flat with thumb and finger
as you sew.

When the purse is embroidered, cut a piece of silk
for a lining just the size of the canvas. Turn under
the ¾-inch seam allowance and baste. Turn under
the canvas seam allowance. Lay the wrong sides
of the lining and canvas together, baste, and overhand neatly around the edges. Now turn up 2¾
inches of the plain end of the strip, and overhand
the sides with raffia (Fig. 8). This forms the pocket,
so be sure to make your stitches close and secure.

In a large purse an interlining of stiff canvas or
buckram will be an improvement. This interlining
is cut just the size of the raffia embroidery, and is
laid on the under side with the cross-stitch canvas
seam allowance folded over the edges and basted
in place. The silk lining is then put on in the way
already described.

The idea of a purse to match a hat is likely to
become very popular when your friends see you
walking down the street with your new purse
under your arm.

Fig. 8   FINISHED PURSE

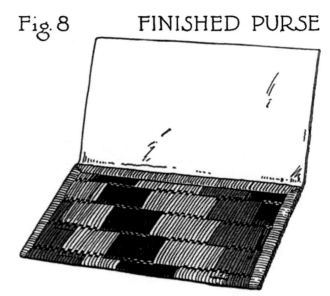

EMBROIDERING STRAW WITH RAFFIA

One of the prettiest decorations for a sun hat is a wreath of raffia flowers and leaves in different colors. It is embroidered flat on the hat around the crown and extends up on the crown and out on the brim. Late in the spring a kind of dark grass sun hat is to be found in the five-and-ten-cent store. A wreath of rose color and lavender daisy-like flowers with yellow and orange centers, and leaves in two shades of green, is lovely with this grass-like straw. If you prefer to use an old hat of your own you will find it quite transformed by this wreath. It is easier to push a needle through a fairly open straw. Peanut straw is easily handled, but Milan straw is too closely woven for this work.

If the hat is colored, a wreath of natural-color raffia daisies with a few small yellow flowers and green leaves may be prettiest. The stitches for these flowers are very simple and should be done a bit loosely. Part of the good effect is due to the irregular length of stitch in the flower petals. The flowers and leaves of any design should be sketched

✤ STITCHES ✤ and MOTIFS for RAFFIA EMBROIDERY

on the hat with pencil, or with crayons, if you prefer. The crayons may be in the colors you intend using for the design.

In drawing the design a single line is enough for a stem or flower petal. See the band designs for the lines on which leaves and flowers are to be embroidered. These show how to draw the pattern around the hat. First place the middle stem line at the meeting of crown and brim. Next draw the flowers an equal distance apart. Last of all draw the lines for leaves.

Do not worry if your lines are a bit crooked and uneven. The raffia covers them, and leaves and petals are prettier if uneven in length.

With a band design it is often pretty to add a cluster of two or three flowers with leaves near the front of the crown, close to the band.

Flowers and leaves are worked from the outside edge toward the center. Flower centers may be a group of little cross-stitches placed close together, or they may be made of stitches crossed and re-crossed many times, or of stitches laid close together

✤ HATS ✤ EMBROIDERED in RAFFIA

to make a solid spot of color. Stems or grasses are done in outline stitch.

These same flowers make pretty decorations on the woven straw envelopes which may be found in five-and-ten-cent stores. A blanket stitch of colored raffia trims the edge and a little nosegay of raffia flowers is worked on one side. Rose color, lavender, green, yellow, and orange, are good colors to use with these greenish envelopes. See the diagram for suggestions of design.

A lining of light-colored silk for the inside half of the straw envelope would make a pretty finish. For this lining measure the length and the depth of the piece to be lined. Cut a piece of the lining material the length of the envelope and twice the depth, allowing a seam on all sides. To make the lining pocket, double the material wrong side out and sew the ends in a seam. Turn the edge over the depth of a seam on the wrong side of the material, and baste in place. Slip this lining pocket inside the straw envelope, and catch it in position around the edge of the envelope with a basting thread. The prettiest way to hold this silk in place is to blanket-stitch the edges of straw and lining with raffia, using the same color of raffia as you used for the blanket stitching on the outside of the envelope.

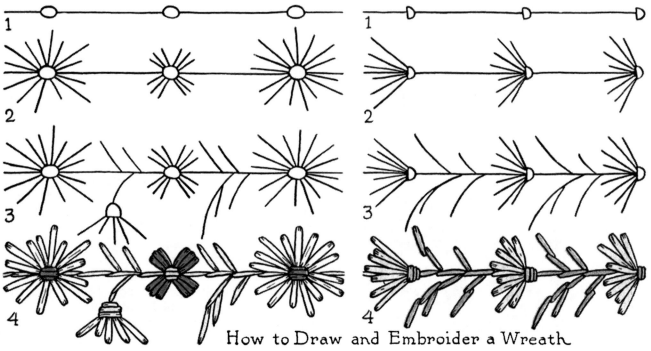

How to Draw and Embroider a Wreath

A SAMPLER

Materials: A 13-inch square of linen or scrim, a 12-inch square of cross-stitch canvas, embroidery cotton

When Great-Grandmother was your age she was, without a doubt, making a cross-stitch sampler. Perhaps you have seen the very one. In those days making a sampler was part of a girl's education. Samplers were supposed to show samples of different stitches and patterns, besides being samples of the maker's skill. Later they came to be entirely of cross-stitch, with carefully arranged designs in many colors. These made beautiful wall decorations. Often they had a cross-stitched verse which did not sound much like one a little girl would choose today.

A favorite verse for samplers was this:

"When I was young and in my Prime
You see how well I spent my Time.
And by my Sampler you may see
What care my Parents took of me."

One child embroidered this on her sampler:

"Please to survey this with a tender eye
Put on good nature and lay judgement by."

A very old sampler had this verse:

"Delight in Learning Soon doth Bring
A Child to Learn the Hardist Thing."

Work from left to right on the wrong side.

1 First take up about 4 threads on needle.

2 Then take a stitch through the folded edge of the hem.

Right side of Hemstitching

The spelling, you see, was not always as perfect as the stitches!

There are not enough old samplers for everyone nowadays, but it would be fun to make one all your own for the wall of your room. Your materials are embroidery cotton and a piece of scrim or linen canvas of very open weave so that threads are counted easily. Or you may use cross-stitch canvas basted over a piece of linen. Ivory or cream-colored linen is prettier than white. Some of the old samplers were cross-stitched on a golden-tan linen scrim which makes a very good background color, too. If you have the right kind of material in plain white, you can make it a beautiful creamy color by boiling it in black tea.

The samplers shown in the illustration are smaller than Great-Grandmother's and are worked in larger stitches, so they are more easily made, and working them is not hard on the eyes as the working of many of the old ones must have been. They are shown as suggestions for arrangement. You can select your own group of motifs from those illustrated here, so that your sampler will be unlike any other.

The alphabet sampler is a usual style, and, to be more complete, it may have the numerals, too. (See page 11.) The other arrangements are purely decorative. In grouping the cross-stitch designs it is well to follow some general scheme. A sampler with a house and fence, a prim-looking tree, birds, dogs, and people will be quaint. A sampler with birds and flowers is pretty too. Maybe you will like to divide your sampler into little bands and squares with alphabets and borders for the design, and only a small spot or two of pattern for contrast.

Each of the samplers illustrated is 12 inches square when hemmed. This requires a 13-inch square of material cut by a drawn thread. The hems are folded about ¼ inch deep, basted, and hemmed before starting the cross-stitch. If your material is an open weave you can hemstitch the hem without pulling a thread, but do not try to take up more than two or three threads at a time. A colored thread used for hemstitching gives a pretty effect. The diagram shows the method of hem-stitching with colored thread. When the hem is done, fold the opposite sides together and crease, then fold the opposite corners together and crease. In this way you find the center lines and the exact center of the square.

If you use cross-stitch canvas baste it on exactly to cover the sampler except for the hems. It is creased just as the linen has been creased.

First select a border you think is suitable for the general plan you intend to carry out. If you have not done much cross-stitch it is best to choose a simple border. The border in two colors on the Bird Sampler is an easy one, and the House Sampler border in one color is a border which is even easier to make.

If the border design is a narrow one, it may be started at a corner, and continued around the sampler. The best way to turn the corners is to work the design the same on both sides of the diagonal crease.

If the border design is a wide one, like the border on the Bird Sampler, it is better to place the design so that it is the same on both sides of the middle creases. To do this, start the border at the middle of each side, in the center of one section of the design, and work to the corner. The second half of each side is worked in the opposite direction, of course. The creases help you to place the parts of your design. First put in the larger and more important parts at center top and bottom, then put in those at the corners. Fit in the smaller motifs where they look best, on one side. Then by measuring and creasing horizontally, place the motifs on the other side of the sampler to match.

The colors you select for the cross-stitching have a great deal to do with the attractiveness of your sampler. Most of the old samplers are done in several colors. Any of the designs shown may be embroidered in two colors, or in more colors if you wish.

In planning a House Sampler in which the house, trees, and grass are important, choose colors for these first. A good medium-dark green for the trees and a lighter green for the grass and the vine around the tree, with a house the color of pink or yellow brick, make a good start on the color scheme.

If the linen square is dark in color, a white house is better. Green blinds and fence are good for any of these schemes, and a gray or blue roof and front steps. Plan to use these colors in the other parts of the design, adding one or two more colors, such as heliotrope, yellow, and perhaps blue. Be careful to try all the colors together to see that they blend well.

The designs on the Bird Sampler are taken from old Pennsylvania-Dutch door towels which are another form of sampler.

These door towels were long towels decorated with cross-stitch. The designs were placed farther apart than on the samplers, and sometimes the towels were trimmed with fringe or hand-made lace. They were hung on doors, not for use, but as decorations, and very lovely decorations they made. The cross-stitch was usually in two colors: red and dark blue, red and green, or red and black.

Perhaps you would like to use one of these color schemes for your Bird Sampler. Plenty of space is left for your monogram and a date. These may be framed artistically in a line of colored cross-stitch if you wish.

Pulling the canvas threads out after the cross-stitching is done is the most exciting part of the work. These threads are easily drawn from one side of the sampler. The threads running in the other direction are pulled afterward.

When your sampler is done, if the colors are too raw to be harmonious, try dipping the whole sampler in tea. This will tint them enough to make the whole effect harmonious.

When you have completed a sampler you will be experienced enough to try these designs on other articles. It is quite easy to copy cross-stitch designs on paper squared off by blue lines. Stationers carry this paper in sheets or in pads. If you have some, you can start a collection of designs by copying what you may find in books and magazines. A pencil outline of the design filled in with colored crayon is quickly made. Peasant embroideries have many beautiful cross-stitch patterns, and their colors will give you some good ideas for your work. There are sure to be books in your public library that will show you these. If you tell your librarian what you are looking for, she will be glad to help you find it.

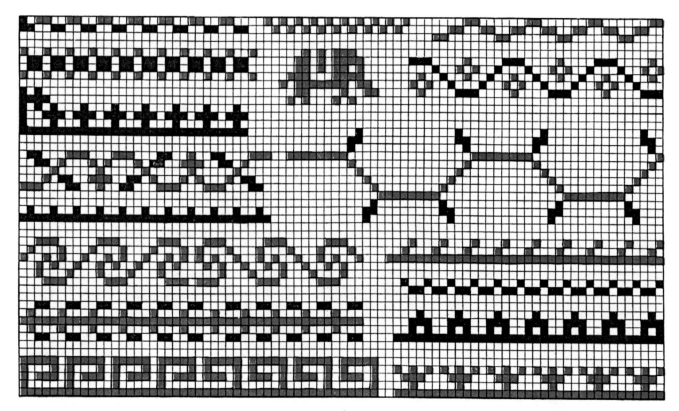

A DOLL'S LUNCHEON SET

Material: One-fourth yard of cotton crêpe

Though this luncheon set is made for your doll, the directions are just the same for a set for Mother, if you use the measurements given for the large set. Perhaps mother's piece bag will hold a bundle of cotton-crêpe pieces that will do for a doll's set. A white set is pretty and a colored set is even prettier. If you have a choice of colors, you will find that yellow is the prettiest, as it gives a cheerful effect and makes a good background for nearly all kinds of flowers and china. Pale green is pretty too. Just see what a charming table you can arrange when your set is all done.

If you buy material, ¼ yard of crêpe 30 inches wide will make a runner, six place mats, and six napkins. The mats are 4 inches long and 3 inches wide, the napkins are 4 inches square, and the runner is 4 inches wide and as long as the width of the doll's table.

Since the edges are fringed, care must be taken to cut them by a drawn thread so they will be perfectly even. But if the set is made from whole cloth it may be torn by first snipping along the selvage for two 4-inch strips, then pulling these apart with a quick jerk. Figure 1 shows the method of dividing the two strips. After tearing or cutting all the pieces apart, trim any selvage edges very close to the edge. Now, ⅜ inch from each edge, near the corner, carefully pick up a thread and gently draw it out. A quick pull is apt to break it. Draw a second thread next to the first.

When you have drawn threads near all edges you are ready for sewing. With a needle and fine thread overhand the inside edge around the rectangle inclosed by the drawn threads (Fig. 2), taking care not to sew through the outside edge. Your stitches should take up about two or three threads in depth. If your thread matches the color of your material, the stitches will not show. This overhanding prevents the crêpe from raveling deeper than you wish, as it is sure to do after use, unless sewed.

Fringe each piece after you finish overhanding it by raveling off the threads from the edge in as far as the overhanding. The first few threads pull off easily. The last threads will pull easily from the end, especially on a large set with deeper fringe.

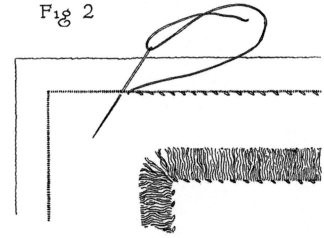

Fig 2

Fig. 1

	4 in.						
MAT	MAT	MAT	NAPKIN	NAPKIN	NAPKIN	NAPKIN	NAPKIN
MAT	MAT	MAT	NAPKIN	RUNNER			

←—3 in.—→ ←—4 in.—→ Make as long as width of doll's table

A LUNCHEON SET FOR MOTHER

Materials: Cotton crêpe, embroidery cotton, cross-stitch canvas

Mother's luncheon set will require 2⅜ yards for four mats, four napkins, and a runner. The mats measure 11 inches by 15 inches, the napkins are 15 inches square, and the runner is 15 inches wide and 50 inches long.

Figure 3 shows how the material is divided for the luncheon set.

Mother would like her cotton-crêpe set for breakfast, probably. If you wish, this may consist of a square cloth and four napkins to match, or it may be a tray cloth the size of the tray used for a breakfast in bed, with two napkins to match. The cloth would measure 30 inches square and the napkins 15 inches square. This will require 1¾ yards of crêpe. Figure 4 shows how the material is torn for the breakfast set.

The fringe on the napkins and cloth should be ¾ inch wide.

It would be fun to do a bit of cross-stitch in one corner of each napkin. Figure 5 shows two little cross-stitch birds worked over canvas in embroidery cotton, either three-strand or a single twist. If your crêpe is colored, the birds may be worked in a lighter or darker shade of the same color, or in white. If the crêpe is white, a soft blue or green would be a good choice for the birds. Use canvas coarse enough to make about eight cross-stitches to an inch. You may like to use a different pattern, but if you do, be careful to count the cross-stitches to reckon the size, for it should not be larger than the bird design shown in Figure 5, which is fourteen squares across in each direction.

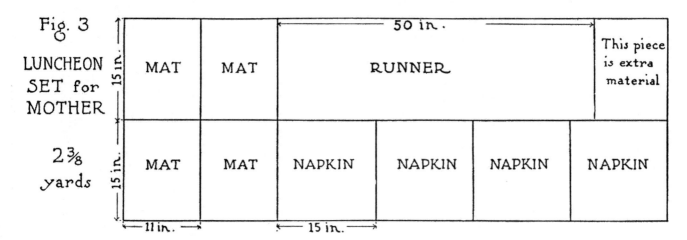

Fig. 3

LUNCHEON SET for MOTHER

2⅜ yards

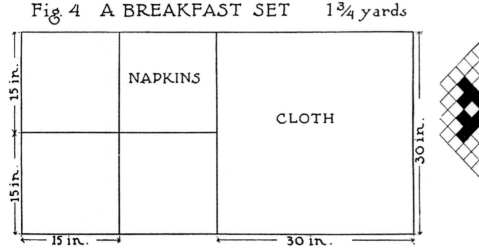

Fig. 4   A BREAKFAST SET   1¾ yards

Fig. 5

TIED-AND-DYED WORK

HAVE you ever seen any tied-and-dyed work? It is a very old way of making a plain material interesting and colorful. In China, Japan, and other oriental countries it is still used, and now it has become popular here. When you have done your first piece of tied-and-dyed work you will be as enthusiastic as is everyone else who has done some of this fascinating work.

The material is tied with a string, sometimes over the end of a stick, or over some object such as a bead or a marble. It is then dyed. After rinsing, the string is untied. Wherever the string has held the folds of material the dye will not have reached, and a softly shaded, irregular spot will be left on the colored material. The shape of the spot depends on the way the string has been wound and tied, and on the shape of the stick. You can never tell just how the pattern will look when done, for no two results are exactly the same. This is one of the interesting things about tied-and-dyed work. Another reason why you will like it is that you can get beautiful colors and patterns by using the plainest and cheapest materials. There are many uses for tied-and-dyed work, and for a number of these the cheapest materials look the best.

Handkerchiefs are a good thing to start with, for they are easily handled. They are so pretty that you will wish you had made more!

TIED-AND-DYED HANDKERCHIEFS

Material: Voile or handkerchief linen

These little handkerchiefs are as dainty and colorful as a flower garden, and the making of them is great fun. It is a good plan to experiment a bit first, before you use new handkerchief linen. Mother is pretty sure to have a discarded dress or bundles of pieces that will supply all the material you will need for experimenting. White or light-colored voile and handkerchief linen both are good for handkerchiefs. When you buy new material for making gifts you will find that a yard of handkerchief linen will make nine handkerchiefs 12 inches square.

The edges of the handkerchiefs should be finished before dyeing, so that the stitches will be dyed to match. After trimming off all selvages, cut 12-inch squares of material by first drawing a thread for straight edges. Cut three or four handkerchiefs, at least, so that you will be able to try out several different schemes of decoration. The edges may be rolled and hemmed, or whipped; or they may have

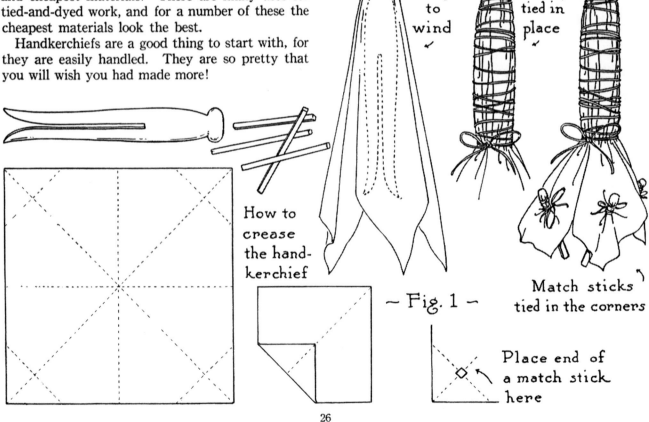

How to crease the handkerchief

Ready to wind

Clothespin tied in place

— Fig. 1 —

Match sticks tied in the corners

Place end of a match stick here

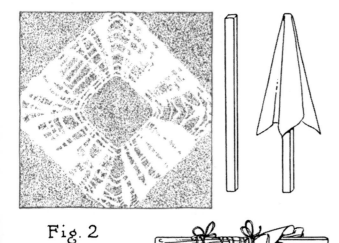

Fig. 2

How to use a square stick

tiny handmade ⅛-inch hems, as many French handkerchiefs do. Have you learned to roll and whip? Look at the chart (page 56) for diagrams of rolling and whipping.

Remember always to roll toward you, from right to left, keeping the edge rolled about an inch and a half ahead of your needle. If you have a hard time starting the roll, moisten your thumb very slightly. Care must be taken to roll the edge evenly by the thread of the material. Corners need a tiny snip of material taken from the roll before rolling the next side. Sometimes these rolled edges are hemmed with very fine thread instead of being whipped.

TYING THE HANDKERCHIEFS

Material: Cotton string

No mention has been made of the various articles used for tying in the handkerchiefs, for there is no rule to be followed. A clothespin makes a lovely cobwebby circle, and this is selected for the first handkerchief.

Crease a hemmed square diagonally, then open and fold it into quarters. Fold up the corners about 2¾ inches and crease (Fig. 1). Open the handkerchief and place the head of an old-fashioned clothespin directly under the center mark, then pull the material down snugly, holding it with the left hand.

Take a piece of cotton string and start winding around the head tightly but openly from right to

left, holding one end of the string in the left hand. This gives you two ends to tie when the winding is finished, about an inch from the end of the clothespin. This way of holding the string is a very important thing to remember in all tied-and-dyed work.

Do not wind regularly. The diagram in Fig. 1 shows how to obtain the best results, by winding closely at two or three points, and very openly at other points, leaving uneven spaces between. Be sure, however, to pull the string snugly, and tie it securely.

To decorate the corners, tie the square end of a match stick in the middle of each corner crease. This makes the small squares shown in the illustration (Fig. 1).

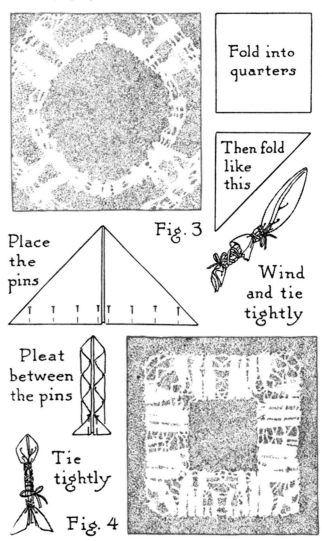

Fold into quarters

Then fold like this

Wind and tie tightly

Fig. 3

Place the pins

Pleat between the pins

Tie tightly

Fig. 4

Now for another way of tying. Put a long square stick in the center of a square, with the corners of the square end pointing toward the sides of the handkerchief. Hold down the folds and wind, leaving a large open center (or a small one if you prefer). This may be wound in two places, for variety (Fig. 2).

Another way is to fold the handkerchief and tie the folds with string. This may be done in various ways. One way is to fold the handkerchief into quarters, then once more, diagonally. Tie around the corners to make large decorated corners, and tie again to make another line inside the handkerchief hem (Fig. 3).

A fourth way to tie is to fold the handkerchief in half, then, with the folded edge away from you, fold over the upper corners to meet on the lower edge, as in the diagram. Now pin in position with pins pointing up and down an inch apart and pleat together in your fingers as evenly as you can. Hold the pleated handkerchief firmly while you pull out the pins. Begin winding a little distance from the center, and wind almost to the edge of the handkerchief. This makes an effect very different from the others you have made. If tied on the extreme edge of the handkerchief, this forms a border of light tone or white.

Dried peas, marbles, and sticks of various shapes, or gathering threads run around the material in a pattern, then tied, all produce any number of interesting variations.

The tied handkerchiefs are all put to soak in warm water to make sure the dye will penetrate the fabric thoroughly. Ten or fifteen minutes is long enough for thin materials to soak, but heavier materials should be soaked longer.

DYEING THE HANDKERCHIEFS

Materials: Good-sized kettle, saucepan and spoon (of tin or granite), two long smooth sticks, wire strainer, old muslin, dye for cotton and linen, newspapers, measuring cup

The dyes you use may be any of the commercial dyes for cotton and linen. You can buy them at a drug store. Ask the druggist to let you see a color card of dyes for cotton and linen, then you can choose your color. Remember that any of the colors may be made much lighter than the color sample. If you buy more than one color it is a good plan to get blue, red, and yellow, for these may be mixed to make other colors.

While the handkerchiefs are soaking you can collect the materials for the dyeing process which must take place in the kitchen or laundry. You will need a tin or granite preserving kettle large enough to float the articles to be dyed; two long smooth sticks for stirring and lifting the material in the dye; a tin or granite saucepan, holding about a quart, in which the dye is dissolved; a tin or granite spoon; a wire strainer, and a bit of old muslin. These things are hard to clean thoroughly, so it is a good plan to use old utensils which may be kept just for dyeing, for you are likely to try other experiments in tie-dyeing.

It pays to be very neat and careful about the dyeing. Put on a large old apron that dye will not spoil, and which will cover you from chin to toes; roll your sleeves out of harm's way, and spread newspapers on the floor and table where you will work. You may not spill a drop of dye, but it is better to be prepared. Now open your package of dye and pour it all into the basin, taking care not

UTENSILS for DYEING

Measure water into kettle | Dissolve and strain the dye into kettle | Stir the cloth in the dye

to shake it, for dye is apt to fly up into the air and around the room. Moisten the dye with a little cold water and stir. Pour in a quart of boiling water and stir to dissolve the dye. Put the large kettle on the stove and fill with enough water to float the articles to be dyed, measuring it as you put it in. Four cups make a quart; four quarts make a gallon. Let the water come to a boil.

While the water is heating put in a heaping tablespoon of salt to a gallon of water. This sets the dye in cotton or linen goods. Then pour in some of the dissolved dye through a piece of muslin placed in the strainer. This will keep any lumps out of the dye bath. When the water is boiling dip a bit of material into it to test the strength of the dye. If, after being in a few minutes, the material is the shade you wish your handkerchiefs to be, it is safe to drop the tied handkerchiefs, squeezed from their first bath, into the dye. If too light, add more dye. Once the pieces are in they must be stirred and turned to keep the color even. If they are allowed to lie unstirred they will be mottled with darker spots. When you think they are dyed dark enough, water may be added to the dye bath, and dye dipped out, to weaken the color. To make the color fast, articles must be boiled 30 minutes in the dye and cooled 30 minutes, stirring them in

the dye all the time. It is not so much skill as patience that makes the color even and fast.

After the cooling process all the dyed articles are rinsed until the last rinsing water shows very little color. Squeeze the articles out of this, then untie them, and shake out. While still damp, press them smooth with a hot iron over several layers of old cloth so that no trace of dye will reach the cover of the ironing board.

When it is not important that the article you make shall be fast color, it need not be boiled quite as long, but the rinsing must be very thorough.

It pays to dye several articles at once, as you can see. Perhaps you will wish to tie a cushion cover or two before you start dyeing handkerchiefs, so that all may be dyed together.

All the unused dye which has been dissolved before starting the dyeing, should be carefully saved for future use. As you use other colors you will be able to mix dyes to make other hues. Some of these colors are far prettier than those you can buy. A yellow dye is improved by adding a very little orange or red dye. Green dye becomes more useful for many things when blue is added to make it blue-green. Blue-green is a very good color for curtains and cushions. A purple dye is never as pretty as when mixed with red or with blue.

Rinse the cloth well | Untie strings | Press the cloth with a hot iron

TIED-AND-DYED CUSHION COVERS

Materials: Unbleached muslin, embroidery cotton
    or tape, dyeing materials

These cushion covers are gay and pretty for
porches, summer cottages, or for the house, and,
what is more, you will like making them. It is not
necessary to have the best quality of unbleached
muslin. The cheap, thin quality is easier to handle
and it looks quite as well. The 40-inch width is
good for cushions because it cuts to good advantage.
A 20-inch length of this 40-inch material makes one
cushion cover. If you buy 1¼ yards you will have
enough to make two cushion covers, unless they are
boxed. Some cushions have the two sides joined
by a narrow strip instead of being sewed together
(see the illustration). These are called boxed
cushions. Allow 6 inches more of length for the
boxing on each cushion. This will make two 3-inch
strips. When pieced together, these strips will
be long enough to go around the sides of the
cushion, forming the boxed edge.

The dyeing is done before the cushion is sewed,
so the tying is the first step after tearing two 20-inch
squares (or whatever the size of your pillow may
be) and the boxing strip, if needed, for each pillow.
You may wish to make two cushion covers. If you
do, you can try out two schemes of decoration at
the same time.

There is no set rule for the tying. Let us plan
two cushion tops—one with a square design and
one with a circle.

A square stick tied in the exact middle of one
square of cloth, with uneven intervals in tying, will
make a handsome and striking pattern. Tie a
clothespin in each corner if you wish to vary the
pattern.

The other cushion cover is just folded and tied
with strips of the muslin and pieces of string that
cover up part of the material very thoroughly, but
allow a large part of the center to be dyed. The
diagram shows the method. Use the strings for
tying near the center, and the strips of muslin
toward the outside edge of the pillow.

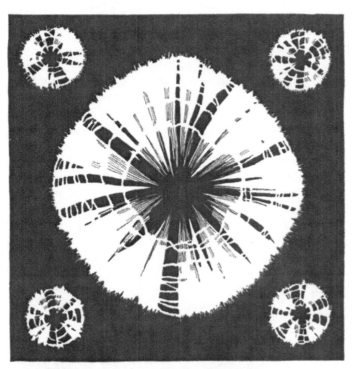

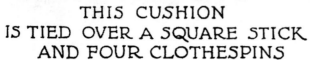

THIS CUSHION
IS TIED OVER A SQUARE STICK
AND FOUR CLOTHESPINS

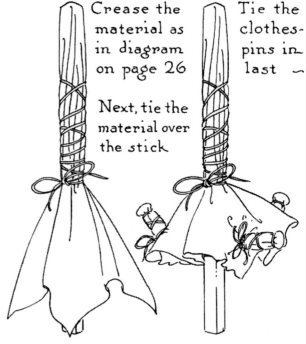

Crease the material as in diagram on page 26

Next, tie the material over the stick

Tie the clothespins in last

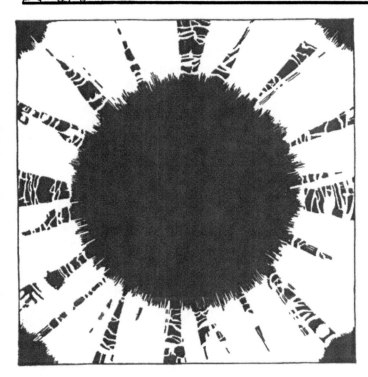

THIS CUSHION IS TIED WITH STRING AND A STRIP OF CLOTH

Fold the material as in Fig. 3 on page 27 →

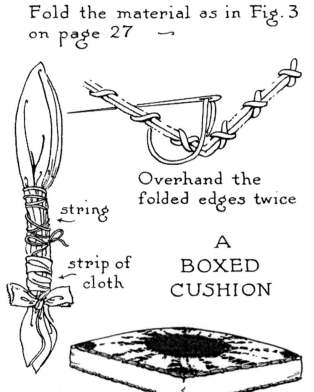

string

strip of cloth

Overhand the folded edges twice

A BOXED CUSHION

Have you thought of colors to use? An orange pillow bound in yellow would be pretty, and so would a blue one bound in bright red or orange. A green pillow bound in orange will be gay, too. Or, if you wish, the pillow may be dyed gray but bound very brilliantly. Your choice, of course, depends on where the pillow is to be used.

When the tying is completed, the pillow tops and the rest of the material for making the covers must be soaked in warm water for at least one hour. The dyeing is done just as for the handkerchiefs, but a large kettle for dyeing is necessary as the material is heavier and there is more of it. When the dyeing and rinsing process is completed, let the article hang until nearly dry, then press with a hot iron.

SEWING THE CUSHION COVERS

Be sure your cover is just the size to fit the cushion, with seams allowed. If the sides of the cushion are boxed, tear two strips the width of the boxing with two seams allowed, and piece together. Seam this around the sides of the top and the back of the cover, on the right side of the material, clipping the strip the depth of the seam at each corner so it will turn neatly. Leave open one side of the boxing and cushion back for slipping in the pillow. Sew this together in a seam when the pillow is in, and bind all the seams with colored tape or bias-fold tape sewed on with running stitch in thread of the same color, making one sewing hold both sides of the binding, and pushing your needle straight through from one side to the other. The same method may be used for cushion covers without the boxing by omitting the strips.

Another way, and one that will be easier, is to turn under and crease the edges of the top, back, and boxing strip (if there is one), then baste together about $\frac{1}{4}$ inch from the edge.

Take heavy embroidery cotton or yarn in a contrasting color and overcast the edges together twice in opposite directions to make the stitches cross on the edge, making your stitches on the line of the bastings. Of course, the pillow must be put in before the fourth side of the cushion cover is sewed together.

A TIED-AND-DYED LUNCHEON SET

Materials: Two and three-eighths yards of unbleached muslin or other material, tying and
dyeing materials

When you have made tied-and-dyed handkerchiefs
and cushion covers you are experienced enough to
make many other things. A luncheon or breakfast
set of tied-and-dyed unbleached muslin is very
pretty, made in the color that will look most charming with the china and glassware. The soft creami-
ness of unbleached cloth gives a much softer color
effect for this work than a dead white material would
do. A tinted cotton crêpe will give a very pretty
effect too, but the muslin is much cheaper than the
crêpe.

The directions for the fringed cotton-crêpe set
are all that you need to make a muslin set. The
sewing and fringing should be done before the pieces
are tied and dyed. Be sure to soak all the tied
pieces thoroughly before dyeing them, and be careful to drop all the pieces into the dye bath together
so the color will be of even depth on all of them.

The size of the spots of design will have to be
planned according to the shape and size of the
pieces, and the way they will look on the table. For
example, a place mat should have the decoration
arranged to look attractive whether or not a plate
is covering the center of the mat. A corner decoration is advisable, and a large center spot is pretty
with the corner decoration, though not as necessary.
A large tied design in the middle of a runner will be
effective. All the help you need in tying and dyeing
will be found in the preceding directions for handkerchiefs and cushion covers.

You will think of many more uses for tied-and-
dyed work. Remember that old discarded dresses
in white or plain colors furnish splendid material
for experiments. The results will often be quite as
lovely as though new materials were used. Old
crêpe de Chine, pongee, and georgette make gay
scarfs, pillow covers, handkerchiefs, and material
for covering shades for lights. Old linen dresses
provide good material for luncheon sets and pillow
covers.

Of course all silks must be washed thoroughly with
a mild soap and water before using, while linen and
cottons need a naptha-soap scrubbing. Remember
that silk requires a different dye from that used for
cotton and linen.

A RAG DOLL

Materials: A stocking, three buttons, yarn, cotton
for stuffing, colored crayons

Did you ever have a rag doll? They are such
soft, cozy little things that one is apt to love them
more than the prettier members of a doll family.
Your small brother or sister will be delighted with a
rag dolly, but I think you will want this one yourself. I have one, and I call her Dulcy. When I
made her there was only one button in my button
bag that was just right for an eye, so I sewed it on,
and later tried to buy another one like it. If there
is one like it I have never found it. After a while
I became so fond of Dulcy as she was that I did not
want to change her at all. A second eye, I thought,
might change her expression from the one I loved.
This is a warning to you! If you want two eyes on
your dolly it is better to find at once, two that match.

This rag doll is made from a full-sized colored
stocking. The face is covered with a piece of white
or flesh-colored silk stocking. A piece of silk glove
or old silk undervest is just as good for making the
face. The arms, too, may be made of this light
material, if you prefer.

See the diagram for the way to cut the stocking.
First cut off the hem at the top. Measure 10 inches

down from the cut edge and cut straight across the stocking. This 10-inch piece makes all of the doll but the arms and feet. The seam of the stocking is at the side of the doll. Turn the piece wrong side out and lay flat with the seam at the side. Double the sides together and pin in place, then cut a curve at the corner of one end. Open the piece you have cut, and with it still wrong side out, sew a seam across the curved end, using combination stitch. Fasten the thread securely, then turn the piece right side out. In handling the stocking be careful not to stretch the raw edges any more than necessary, as runs are apt to start, especially in silk-stocking material.

Taking great care, stuff in fluffs of cotton until the body is filled 6 inches from the curved seam. Pack the lower part quite firmly to stretch the skirt width. The upper part should be stuffed a little less tightly. Measure down from the upper edge of the stocking leg 3½ inches and run a gathering thread straight around. When this is pulled up so that the neck opening is about 1 inch wide, fasten the thread securely. Wind yarn several times around the body snugly for a high waistline—about 1¾ inches from the gathering thread—and tie the yarn securely in a hard knot.

Run a gathering thread around the top edge, and, before fastening it, stuff in fluffs of cotton until the head is round and firmly packed. Take special care to make the face side smooth and plump. Pull up the thread and fasten it, sewing over and across the cluster of gathers to make them secure and flat as well.

Now our dolly must have arms. The pieces for them are cut on a lengthwise fold of the stocking, with one end rounded as in the diagram. They measure 3 inches long and 1¼ inches wide when folded. Fold wrong side out and sew a seam across the curved end and up the side. Turn right side out and stuff carefully with little wads of cotton until each arm piece is plump. Fold in the top edge ¼ inch and run a gathering thread close to the fold. Pull up the thread until the two sides of the gathered end, held together, measure about ½ inch. Fasten the thread, then overhand the sides together closely. Attach the arms to the body with firm stitches in heavy thread, holding the arm up while sewing the gathered edges to the doll. This conceals the stitches somewhat when the arm is down. Tie the wrists with yarn, just as you tied the waistline.

Cut a piece 2 inches wide and 2½ inches long, with the longer side lengthwise of the stocking material. Fold this piece wrong side out and crosswise of the material. Seam one short side and the long side. Turn right side out and stuff with cotton. Turn in the edges of the open side and overhand together. Wind yarn around the middle of this little oblong cushion and tie a bit tightly to give the effect of two plump feet. With firm stitches catch the feet in position with the folded side toward the front.

Cut out a 3½-inch square of the light silk for the face. Lay this over the front of the head and pin at the sides and across the top. A gathering thread will hold in any fullness under the chin. Trim off the corners, then sew the material in place around the sides.

The eyes are two small, round buttons with four holes. They may be black, blue, or brown, but they should not be larger than ⅜ inch in diameter. If black or brown buttons are used, sew them on with crossed stitches of white thread. If blue buttons are used, black thread will be better. These buttons will prove a great attraction to a baby playing with the doll, so be very sure to sew them on securely with heavy linen thread, carrying the stitches

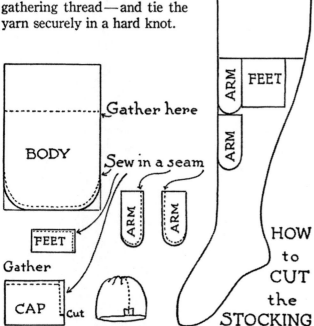

through from the back of the head. A deep pink or a red button makes the mouth. If you have no such button, three stitches of deep pink embroidery cotton will do. Tint the cheeks pink by softly brushing the blunt end of a wax crayon across them. This gives them a smooth, natural color if done carefully. Draw faint eyebrows over the eyes with a pointed brown crayon.

Two small buttons are sewed securely on the front of the waist.

The cap is made from the hem of the stocking. Hold the hem around the head snugly to see how much to cut off. Pin together where the seam will come, then slip off. Allow the width of a seam, and cut through the hem on the straight of the goods. Pin the seam and slip on the head again with the seam at the back. Turn up the folded edge becomingly. Pin the front and back of the cap together, edges even. Slip the cap off again. Cut through the seam at the depth of the turn-back. Trim off all but a narrow seam across the top of the cap. This cap strip will measure about 3 inches wide. Seam up the back on the wrong side, except below the cut. Seam on the right side below the cut. This short seam is covered by the turn-back. Gather the upper edge, bunching the gathers on the inside of the cap. Put the cap on the doll at a becoming angle and so that the raw edges of the face material will be concealed. With the cap in this position pull the turn-back down. Sew the cap to the doll's head with heavy thread along the line to be covered by the turn-back when it is in position. Sew a tuft of yarn at the crown. Tie a narrow ribbon around the neck, with a bow under the chin, and fasten with a few stitches.

A FROCK FOR BELINDA

DOLLS' dressmaking is good fun for a number of reasons. One is that there are so many pieces of beautiful material, too small for anything else, which will make charming doll clothes. Then, too, the seams are all so short that the frock is finished quickly.

Perhaps your doll's name is Hortense or Anne Marie, but, as I do not know what it is, I shall call her Belinda.

Belinda is perfect about keeping very still while being measured and while "trying on." You will understand how much that means to a dressmaker!

It is sometimes hard to find a pattern for a doll exactly Belinda's height, so I am going to tell you how you can cut one, yourself. Then, with this one pattern you can make Belinda several dresses that are quite different.

CUTTING THE PATTERN

Material: Manila paper

This dress is a simple one, and when you have made the pattern you have a foundation for other dresses for Belinda.

The first thing to do is to measure her. The diagram shows you where the tape measure is placed to measure the center-front to the knees, and the center-back to the knees. The measurement from

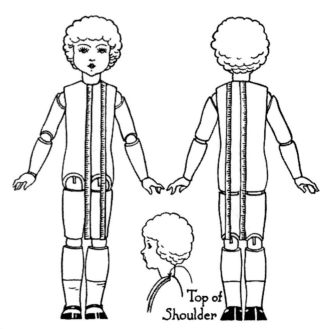

Top of Shoulder

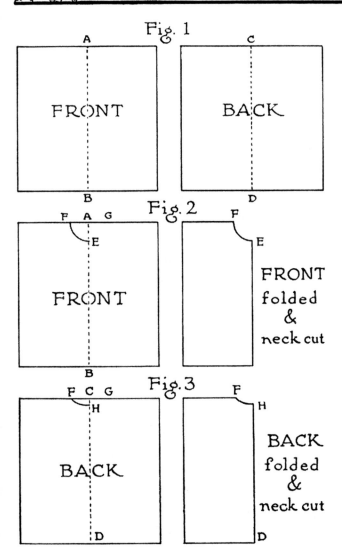

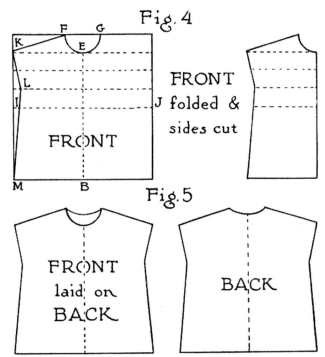

Fig. 1

Fig. 2

Fig. 3

Fig. 4

Fig. 5

FRONT folded & sides cut

FRONT laid on BACK

the top of the shoulder to the knees is made by holding the end of the tape close to the neck on the middle of the shoulder curve. Put a tiny pencil mark on Belinda's shoulder to make sure that the back measurement is taken from the same point.

The difference between the center-front and the top-shoulder measurements gives the depth of the neck opening in front; and the difference between the center-back and top-shoulder measurements gives the depth of the shallow neck curve in the back. Put all these measurements down on paper.

Cut two squares of paper (Fig. 1) with the sides measuring the front top-shoulder to knee distance. Fold each square in half as in the diagram and crease for the center-front and center-back.

Measure down from *A* the depth of the front neck opening, which is *E* (Fig. 2). Measure the same distance out from *A* on each side for *F* and *G*. Draw a curved line connecting *F, E*, and *G*. Fold your paper on the crease and cut out on the pencil line. Open the square and hold up to Belinda's neck to see if the opening is right. If it is too small it may be trimmed out a little. If it is too large, cut a new square and try again, after making sure your measurements are exact. Now lay the two squares of paper with creases together, and mark *F* and *G* on the back where the hollowed-out neck touches the top edge of the paper. Measure down on the center-back crease the depth of the neck in the back (*H*), and draw a shallow curve connecting *F, H*, and *G* (Fig. 3). Fold the paper on *H–D* and cut out on this curved pencil line. Try around Belinda's neck. It should be a comfortable fit, close to the neck.

Take the front square (Fig. 4). Fold the bottom edge up to the top and crease (*I–J*). Open the square. Fold the top edge down to *I–J*, then double the top fold down to *I–J*. Open the square. There are three horizontal creases above *I–J*. The point *K* on the top crease marks the top of the armhole. Draw a line connecting *F* and *K* for the shoulder line. Draw a line slightly slanting as in the diagram, from *K* to the crease above *I–J*. This marks the lowest point of the armhole (L). Connect L and M. Fold the square on E–B and cut on the straight pencil lines.

To cut the back, lay back and front together (Fig. 5) and cut around the sides.

CUTTING OUT THE FROCK

Materials: Linen, cretonne or piqué, white linen tape

This pattern is suitable for a linen, piqué or cretonne frock, for it has no gathers. As it is your first frock it is to be simple to make. Ask mother if you may have a little roll of white linen tape, size 3 (⅜ inch wide), for your sewing box. It will be useful for more than one frock. And perhaps she may have a roll of pieces of linen or piqué left from a frock she has made for you. It will not take very much for Belinda.

To cut the frock, lay your material flat and place your pattern on it so that the center-front and center-back run on the straight of the goods and

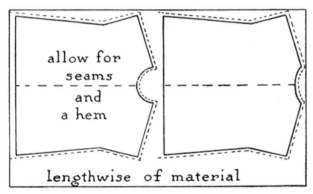

Fig. 6

parallel with the selvage (Fig. 6). No seams are allowed on your pattern, so be sure to allow seams and a hem. The diagram will help you. The seams would be very heavy for a doll if made ⅜ inch wide, as in clothes for yourself. About ¼ inch wide is enough for heavy or closely woven materials like linen and gingham. A hem about 1 inch deep is good, though it need not be so deep if your material is too scant for that.

Grown-up mothers of real children have to plan for letting down hems, but dolls are a real comfort in this respect—they never outgrow their frocks!

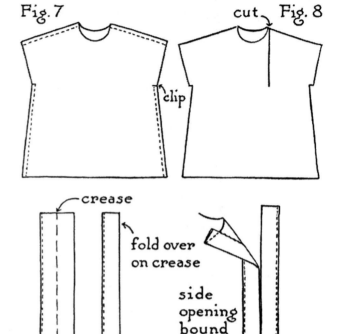

Fig. 7 cut Fig. 8

clip

crease

fold over on crease

side opening bound

Fig. 9 Fig. 10

SEWING THE FROCK

Now lay the back and front together and sew the shoulder seams and side seams in even little stitches, backstitching every four or five stitches. Clip in the depth of the seam at the lower end of the armhole (Fig. 7). Now turn the frock right side out and cut down on the left side of the neck line to a point level with the lower end of the armhole (Fig. 8). Try the frock on Belinda to see if she has room for her head to go through. If the opening is too small, clip a little farther and try again.

Cut two pieces of tape the length of this side opening with a seam allowed. Turn up a seam on the end of each piece of tape and crease the tape down the middle for a guide line in sewing it on. Lay a piece of tape on the right side of the material with the crease of the tape even with the edge of the opening and the turned-under edge at the bottom of the opening. Sew to the frock with running stitch and fine thread. When one tape edge is sewed on the right side, turn the frock inside out and hem the other edge of the tape down neatly on the wrong side. The diagrams (Figs. 9 and 10) will help you. When both tapes are hemmed down,

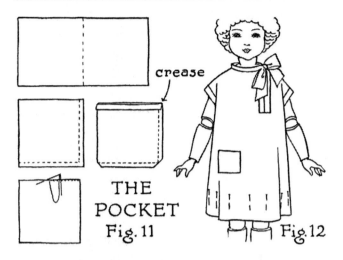

THE POCKET
Fig. 11   Fig. 12

first cutting a little cardboard gauge as wide as the narrow part of the hem and using this to guide your scissors. Turn in the raw edge and baste around with long stitches, then hem with fine thread and small stitches that show as little as possible on the right side of the dress.

ADAPTING THE FROCK PATTERN

Now that you have the pattern for this frock you will find it useful for making other frocks by varying the material and the way of trimming. Here are three ways of using this pattern. Remember that cretonne, linen, and piqué are the best materials for such a plain frock.

Style *A* is just like the frock you have made, with blanket stitching in colored embroidery cotton around the white bindings and pocket. See your chart (page 56) for the way to do blanket stitching, if you do not remember how to do it.

Style *B* opens down the middle of the front. Before binding the neck and sleeves a strip of linen tape is sewed down over each shoulder seam and around the front opening. The corners are "mitered" neatly as in the sketch. The neck and armhole bindings cover the ends of these trimming

catch the corners of the two bindings firmly together at the lower end of the closing with several small stitches, one on top of another, so the opening can not tear down below the binding.

The armholes are bound in the same way. If you are careful to read these binding directions and carry them out perfectly, you will not have to be told about binding with tape again, for you will have learned just how to do it. The neck is bound in the same way except that 5 inches of tape are left hanging from each end of the neck binding for ties.

For a pocket (Fig. 11), cut a small oblong of white linen which is square when folded double. This should be large enough, when the little seams are turned in, for Belinda's hand to be slipped inside. Fold in a square and sew around two sides, creasing the third side over on both edges, but leaving it open. Clip the tiny corners so the pocket will turn neatly, then turn right side out and overcast the open side with small neat stitches. Decide where the pocket should go for Belinda's hand to slip into it conveniently. A pocket usually is placed with its top edge about halfway between the shoulder and the hem edge. Pin in place or catch with a few basting stitches, then hem onto the frock with fine thread and short stitches on the right side but longer ones on the wrong side.

Try the frock on Belinda and turn up the hem. This will not be an even distance all around, probably; it depends on Belinda's figure. Do you see in Figure 12 how the pins are placed up and down to hold the hem? This is the best way to make the edge hang evenly. Now trim off to an even distance,

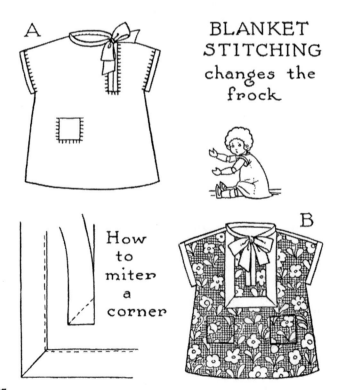

BLANKET STITCHING changes the frock

How to miter a corner

37

tapes. This time, make the pockets of material like the dress.

Style *C* has a little shaped vest of white linen. Cut a pattern first, so the size and shape will please you, then cut it out from linen, allowing a narrow seam. Turn in the outer edge, and baste. Cut the opening as long as for the first frock you made, both in the vest piece and on the dress front. Be very careful to cut straight by the thread of the material. Lay your vest, seams up, on the wrong side of the front (before the back is seamed on the front) with the edges of the openings exactly even. Seam them together, running the seam to a point exactly at the end of the opening, as in the drawing. Turn the front over to the right side and draw the vest through the opening and press flat on the right side. Baste the vest in place and hem it down on the dress, or you may like to blanket-stitch the edge in place with colored embroidery cotton.

The little pockets are cut with rounded corners to match the shape of the vest. They are sewed on the dress in the same way the vest is sewed on it, or blanket-stitched in the same color.

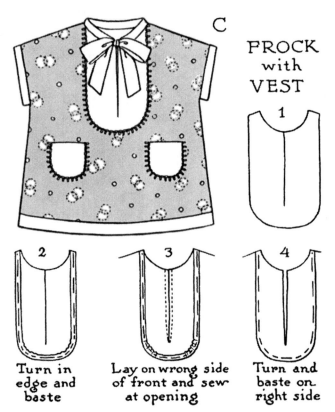

C

FROCK
with
VEST

1

2
Turn in
edge and
baste

3
Lay on wrong side
of front and sew
at opening

4
Turn and
baste on
right side

BELINDA'S SUNBONNET

Materials: White organdie or lawn

Belinda will look charming in this organdie sunbonnet. You will find that the pattern may be used for other bonnets, too. Don't you like bonnets to match frocks? They give a doll such a well-dressed look.

Measure Belinda's head as follows: Hold the end of the tape measure at the line of the eyebrows and draw the tape over the top of the head to the nape of the neck. Write down the measurement. We will call it *A–B*. Now measure the distance from the neck below the ear across the top of the head to the neck below the other ear. Write down this measurement. We will call it *C–D*.

Cut a rectangle of paper measuring *A–B* in width and *C–D* in length. Fold in quarters as in Figure 1.

Open the paper and fold in thirds the other way of the paper (Fig. 2), and letter the points marked in the diagram.

Now fold diagonally from *E* through *F*; fold again from *G* through *H*.

Cut down from *G* to *F* on the fold, then out to the edge of the paper on the diagonal fold as the heavy line of Figure 3 shows. Then cut from *E* to *H* and out to the edge on the diagonal. The pattern looks like Figure 4 and is ready for use.

As the bonnet is of thin material, it must be made of two thicknesses. In cutting, lay the long edge of the pattern on a straight fold, taking care that the material is even in upper and under layers. Pin the pattern in place and cut out, allowing narrow seams on all sides except the folded edge.

Now sew the two layers together from the folded edge to the short straight side opposite the fold (Fig. 5), and clip in at the angles as shown. Take care not to cut your stitches. The clipping is important, for without it the corners will not turn neatly when the bonnet is turned right side out. Now turn the bonnet right side out, pressing the seams flat so the outside fold is smooth and straight. Turn in the edges of the open side and run together with small stitches. Overhand the diagonal edge and the short side of the back together, on both sides of the bonnet.

Now catch together the lower ends of these overhanded edges with a pin and try on Belinda. Lay the back fullness in a pleat on either side and pin in place when the bonnet is put on at the most

Fig. 1   A-B

C-D

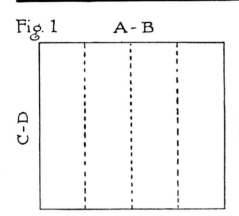

Fig. 2   A-B

G   E

F   H

C-D

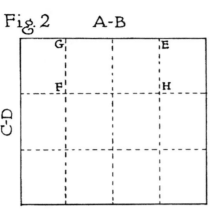

Fig. 3   Pattern

G   E

F   H

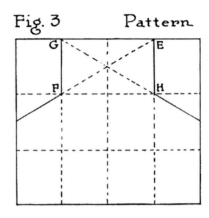

becoming angle. Make tie strings of linen tape about five inches long and attach to the bonnet right under the ears. Mark where the pleats lap and sew a snap fastener on each side to fasten them. This will make it easy to launder the little bonnet. If you prefer to sew the pleats in place, the stitches will have to be ripped for laundering.

This pattern may be varied by cutting duplicates of your first pattern and trying other ideas. One bonnet may be made of cretonne to match a cre-

tonne frock, with a facing of plain colored gingham to match the trimming on the frock. Cut this with rounded sides as in Figure 7.

Another bonnet may be of piqué with bias binding around the edges and no lining at all. The fullness in back might be gathered (Fig. 8).

Still another bonnet may be of silk, with a ribbon band with a flat bow over the top and extending far enough to form a chin strap (Fig. 9). This makes a very "dress-up" bonnet.

Fig. 4

Allow for seams

Pattern pinned on material

This edge on fold

Fig. 5

clip→   ←clip

overhand

Fig. 6

Fig. 7

Fig. 8

Fig. 9

AN APRON FOR YOURSELF

Materials: Three-fourths of a yard of unbleached muslin, colored bias-folded tape, colored embroidery cottons

Making clothes for yourself is not so very different from making clothes for Belinda. There is more sewing to be done, but there is more satisfaction, too. Think of wearing a garment that you have made yourself! An apron is a good thing to make first. You will like this one, for it is so different from most aprons.

The apron is of unbleached muslin. The pattern is very simple, as you can see by the diagram. Just ¾ yard of material is needed for the twelve-year size, and 6 inches less for the six-to-eight-year size. You will need about 3 yards of bias-folded tape ⅝ inch wide.

The embroidery may be done in two colors of cotton embroidery twist. Yellow is a good color for the basket stitches, and yellow daisies with pale green stems and leaves make a pretty combination with deeper blue-green binding. A deep yellow binding would be nice with pale yellow daisies and green basket stitches and stems. A binding of soft blue would look well with lavender daisies, while rose colored bindings would be pretty with pale pink English daisies. To make these pink daisies even prettier, take two little straight stitches of deep pink in the tip of each petal after the flower is embroidered.

To cut the apron, measure off 27 inches of the width of your material and 27 inches of length (for six-to-eight-year size make 6 inches shorter). Tear or cut out this square piece. Fold it lengthwise of the material. Measure down 8 inches on the fold and place a pin. Measure 4 inches straight in at right angles from this pin, and place a second pin. Measure 8 inches down on the side opposite the fold. Clip the material and tear each side in as far as the second pin. Now fold over the muslin from this point to the end of the folded edge, as shown in the diagram. Cut on the slanting fold. This makes the little pointed bib for the front of your apron.

To sew the apron, first fold and baste small hems on the sides of the apron. Hem these, then fold up 2 inches of length for a hem across the bottom of the apron, baste, and hem.

Gather across the top of each side and pull up the gathers to fit a stay strip 4½ inches long. Cut stay strips from a narrow edge torn from the selvage of the unbleached muslin. Baste each stay strip along just above the gathers.

YOUR APRON

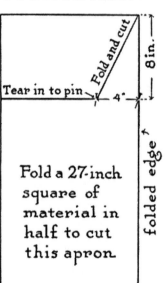

Fold a 27-inch square of material in half to cut this apron.

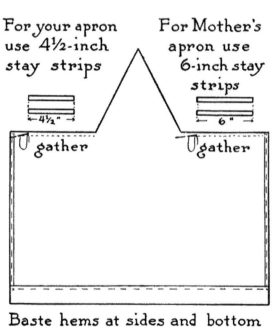

For your apron use 4½-inch stay strips

For Mother's apron use 6-inch stay strips

Baste hems at sides and bottom

MOTHER'S APRON

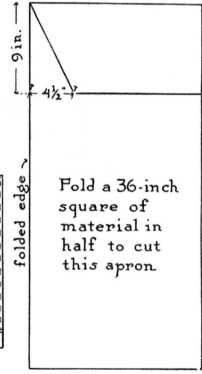

Fold a 36-inch square of material in half to cut this apron.

The next thing to do is to clip a 3-inch and a 4-inch piece from your bias tape to save for the basket decoration. Measure off 22 inches of the tape to leave hanging for a string, then start running on the tape binding. Hold one fold open with the edges even with the muslin edge, and sew on the crease. Hold the tape flat but do not stretch it. Sew in a neat angle at the bib. When the point of the bib is reached, hold the apron against your frock with the gathers at the right level. A pin will keep that part in place while you measure for the neck strap. Pass the tape around your neck and back to the point of the bib. Mark the place on the tape where it meets the bib. Now take off the apron, lay the tape flatly around in a loop, and start basting it on the bib at the pin. When the binding is all sewed once, fold it double and baste, beginning on the tie and working straight around the apron and loop and the other tie. Now hem it all down with colored thread, and overhand the edges of the loop and ties.

The basket is formed by the two pieces of bias binding folded on the straight of the goods at the ends, and hemmed down across the middle of the bib, with embroidery stitches connecting the bias strips. The flowers and leaves are made in lazy-daisy stitch (see chain stitch on page 56) with coarse outline stitch for stems. The long stitches between the bias strips of the basket are made slanting in

This is 1/2   actual size

one direction first, then the opposite slanting stitches are made. Last, take a series of small stitches to catch down the long stitches where they cross each other.

The apron is even prettier with a binding at sides and bottom edge, instead of hems. This is a little more work, but it is worth trying if you are making a very special gift. The diagram for cutting gives measurements for an apron for Mother, too.

A TIED-AND-DYED COOLIE COAT

Materials: Two and a quarter yards of unbleached muslin or challis, dyeing materials

Coolie coats are cut just like the coats worn by the coolies, or porters, in China and Japan. They are loose, comfortable, and easily made. That is why people like to use them for bath gowns, lounging robes, and beach coats. They may be made very gay with bright colors and pattern.

You will like your gay coolie coat for a bath gown or beach coat. As you see by the diagram, the cutting is simple. The dyeing is done before sewing the coat. The diagram allows for a coat 28 inches long from shoulder to hem. If you wish this longer or shorter, you must alter this measurement. You will need 2¼ yards of material 27 inches wide or wider. Challis is narrow and there is no waste; unbleached muslin is 36 inches wide, so a 9-inch side strip is not used.

The first step is to trim off one end of your material so it will be exactly even. Measure across the end 21 inches and tear from this point through the length of your material. Measure off with your tape measure 56 inches on the strip that is 21 inches wide,

THE APRON   FINISHED

flower   leaf

41

and tear across. Measure on the selvage of the short piece, just torn off, for two 12-inch strips, and tear across. Now tear a 6-inch strip the length of the long side strip. If your material is challis this side strip will be exactly 6 inches wide, and no tearing will be necessary. The large piece measuring 56 inches by 21 inches will make the front and back of the coat. The neck and the front opening are not cut until the coat is dyed. The 12-inch pieces are for sleeves, and the long strip is the collar which will edge the front opening.

Now it is time to tie the coat. A big circular motif in the middle of the back, across the shoulders, looks quite oriental. To find the point for the center of this motif, fold the 56-inch piece across the middle, then lengthwise through the middle. Crease so the marks will show. The folded corner marks the center of the neck opening. Measure 8½ inches down on the middle fold from the folded corner and mark with a pin. Open up and place the head of a clothespin under this pin; pull the material down on all sides, and hold it while winding from the head of the clothespin. Wind openly with a fine string most of the distance, and wind closely for ¼ inch in

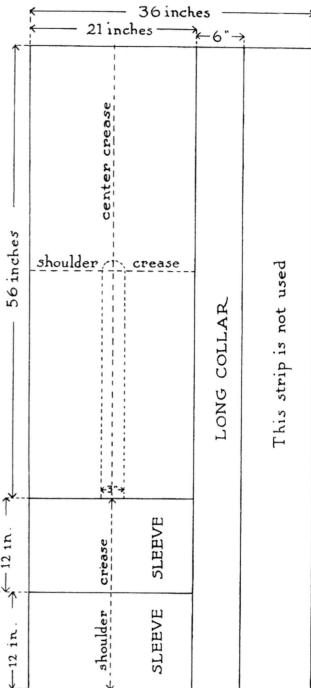

THE
COOLIE COAT
FINISHED

Back View

The front opening is not cut
until the material has been dyed

two places, ½ inch apart, near the end. The tying should not come nearer than 4½ inches to the place marked on the material as the middle of the neck.

There are two clothespin motifs on each sleeve, placed as the diagram indicates. Fold the long collar across the middle and crease. Measure 10 inches from each side of this crease for the point at which the top designs are to be placed. Crease the strip lengthwise through the middle so the design may be placed at one side of the fold. These tied spots must be placed on one side of the fold, as the collar is made double and shows only one side. Use button molds, beads, or little wooden cubes (the cubes will make square spots) for the smaller units of the design.

Be sure to soak the tied pieces an hour or two in warm water, squeezing the water through them when you put them in and when they are taken out. Follow the dyeing directions for tied-and-dyed handkerchiefs, remembering to use plenty of water to float all the pieces at once.

Red, burnt orange, green, and violet-blue (obtained by mixing a little red in the blue dye) are all pretty colors for a coat. Test the dye bath with any scraps of material you may have left. If your coat is of challis the dye must be for wool and silk. If unbleached muslin is used it must, of course, be for cotton. Always read the directions on the package of dye before using.

After rinsing and untying, allow the pieces to hang until nearly dry, then smooth with a hot iron. Now fold the back and front piece together, end to

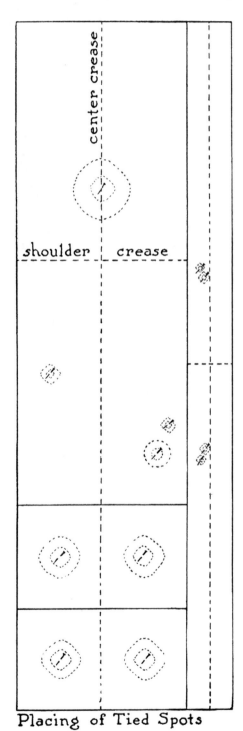

Placing of Tied Spots

end, and crease for the shoulder line. Open and fold lengthwise. Measure from the shoulder crease 1½ inches down on the center fold of the back and mark with a pin. Measure the same distance in from the center fold on the shoulder line and mark with a second pin. Cut a curve between the two pins, then clip on the straight of the goods down the front from the second pin and tear the rest of the way.

Now for sewing! Fold the sleeve strips in half, crosswise, to crease for the top line. Lay the right side of the sleeve on the right side of the coat material, with the top-line crease exactly on the shoulder-line crease. Baste the edges in a seam and then sew together with combination stitch. Join both sleeves to the coat. Lay the front and back of the coat together, right side out, with sleeves extended. Pin the sleeve seams and the sides of the coat evenly, then baste and sew close to the edge with running stitch. Crease the seams open, then turn the coat wrong side out to complete the French seams. Crease the seams neatly, then sew with combination stitch. Fold under a narrow hem around the bottom of the sleeves; baste and hem. Fold a 1-inch hem around the bottom of the coat; baste and hem it.

Now lay the long collar, folded lengthwise, with the plain right side of the strip of material on the right side of the coat, and the exact middle of the strip at the center-back on the neck line. Beginning at the center-back, with the coat resting on a table, pin closely around the neck line, keeping the edges even. Pin down the fronts. Baste the seam, then sew with a running stitch. Turn under and crease the seam on the other edge of the strip, cutting off all but 1 inch of the extra length below the hem. Turn up the inch of material and catch in place. Baste the folded edge even on the line of stitching and hem. Overhand the seams where the sleeves are sewed in, and your coat is done!

This coat also may be made of colored cotton crêpe stenciled or block-printed in a striking design.

A SMOCK

Materials: Colored cotton crêpe, colored thread to match, raglan smock pattern

This may be the first time you have used a ready-made pattern. The differences between this and the patterns you yourself have cut for various things are these: the ready-made pattern has all seams allowed (these are ⅜ inch wide unless there is special mention of a wider seam), and there are helps for putting the garment together, such as notches and printed directions. You see, if you choose very simple styles, the ready-made patterns really are easier to use than your own. In selecting a smock pattern, it would be well to buy a raglan style as it is easy to put together and becoming, too. A raglan sleeve runs up to the neck line and joins the front and back in slightly curved seams.

The amount of material needed for the garment is always given on the pattern envelope, so it is best to buy the pattern first, then choose the material. Cotton crêpe is easy to sew on, but there are other materials quite as suitable for smocks, such as plain colored ginghams, linen, cotton suiting, and figured cretonne. These are a little stiffer and heavier to handle than the crêpe.

The first thing to do is to read all the directions on your pattern. There are always charts to show ways of laying the pattern on the material. Crêpe is about 31 inches wide, so select the chart for narrow fabrics, and follow that.

Lay your material on a table. Fold it very evenly through the middle, lengthwise. Pin along the selvages at intervals to hold from slipping.

Next, lay your pattern on, with special care to put the pattern for the back with the center-back against the folded edge. The collar pattern will probably be cut on a fold, too. Pin the patterns in place, taking care not to overlap any edges, and

pointing your pins at right-angles to the edge of the patterns. It is easier to cut a straight edge with the pins placed in this manner. The collar should be faced, so be sure to cut a second collar of the material, or of white crêpe, if you would like a contrasting facing.

Now cut around each pattern, taking care to follow the edges exactly. Cut all the notches. Before unpinning the pattern use a bit of chalk or soap to mark the perforations for placing pockets, pleats or gathers, and the center-front. Unpin the patterns and before unfolding the material poke a pin through each chalk mark to the other side of the doubled material and mark the place with chalk.

There are two important things to remember in putting the smock together. These are so simple that one is apt to forget them. One is to be sure to make all your seams come on the inside of the smock. The other thing to remember is to hold your work flat as you sew. The easiest way is to sit in front of your table with the work lying on the table near the edge. If you hold it in your lap you are apt to bend over it, tiring your eyes and your back. There is not much fun in sewing that way!

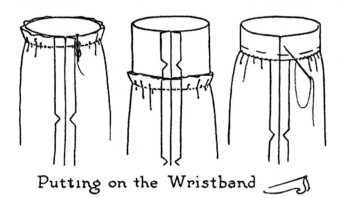

Putting on the Wristband

Now for putting the pieces together. Lay the sleeves on the fronts with notches together, pinning them in place, with the pins pointing in from the edge as when you pinned the paper pattern. Baste the seam, then sew with combination stitch on an even line ⅜ inch from the edge.

Next, pin the sleeves to the backs in the same fashion. Baste and sew as before. Now lay the side seams of the fronts and back together, with the sleeve edges meeting, too. Pin, baste, and sew the seams.

Gather the bottom edges of the sleeves, leaving an end of thread wound on a pin, so the gathers may be adjusted.

Close the ends of the wristbands with combination stitch. Crease the seams open.

Hold the smock sleeve wrong side out for the next work (see the diagram). Turn the wristband with the seam inside and slip inside the gathered end of the sleeve. Pin the edges of sleeve and band together. Hold the band open with your left hand and pull up the gathering thread with your right until it just fits the band. Fasten the thread. Pin the sleeve and band together, after pushing the gathers along evenly, then baste closely, and sew in a seam with plenty of backstitches. Now pull the band out and crease over the edge ⅜ inch. Pin this folded edge down over the raw edges to the line of gathers. Baste and hem the edge down.

When both sleeves are done, turn back the hems on the fronts. Pin, baste, and hem them. Now lay the two layers of collar together and join them with a basting. Sew the ends and outer curve in a seam, backstitching now and then to keep the edge from stretching. Notch the outer curve by folding the edge and clipping the fold not quite as far as the line of stitching. This makes the edge curve

evenly when the collar is turned. Turn the collar right side out and baste the outer curve neatly.

Lay the collar on the right side of the smock, with notches together, and pin in place. Baste, then sew in the usual ⅜-inch seam. Now lay bias-fold tape around the entire neck opening on the right side of the smock. Open one side of the tape and sew on this crease over the line of stitching on the collar. Leave a bit of the tape to turn under on each end.

Snip in nearly to the stitching every ½ inch, all around the neck curve, then turn the tape under to cover the raw edges. Lay it flat, then baste in place, turning under the ends even with the front edge of the smock. Hem this down, using thread the color of the smock so no stitches will show on the right side.

Try on the smock to see if it needs to be turned up farther than the pattern directs. Cut a cardboard gauge the width of the hem needed and, after turning under a narrow edge all around, pin up an even hem. It is best to pin first at center-front, center-back, and side seams, then to work between these points.

The pockets come next. Turn in and baste ⅜ inch on the sides and across the bottom. Turn the hem across the top; baste and hem it. Place the pockets where the chalk marks indicate, and baste in place. Hem down closely with very short stitches on the right side, and longer ones underneath.

The smock may be fastened with snap fasteners or with buttons and buttonholes. If buttons are used, only the plainest style of button is suitable. If snap fasteners are used, be sure to put the smaller part of the fastener on the under-lap. The right side should lap over the left on a girl's smock.

When you have learned to use a sewing machine you will be able to make a smock much more quickly, but making one by hand will be a great help to you in later work with the machine.

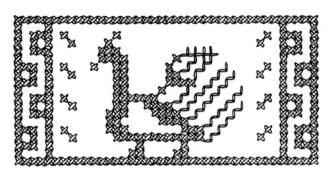

SEWING CHART

Running stitches should be even in size. Three or four may be taken on the needle before pulling the thread through.

Backstitch is made as in this illustration. The thread is carried ahead of each stitch, then the needle is stuck in exactly at the end of the last stitch.

Basting stitches are long running stitches to hold material in place for sewing or pressing.

Combination stitch consists of one backstitch and two or more running stitches. It is stronger than plain running stitches and prevents stretching.

Overcasting is done from left to right. It keeps raw edges from raveling.

Overhanding is used to join two folded edges or selvages.

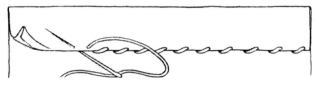

Hemming holds a folded edge in place. Hold the hem over the forefinger with the folded edge to the right. Take small slanting stitches.

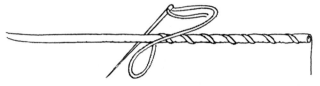

Rolling and whipping is done by rolling the edge of the material toward you and overcasting the roll evenly.

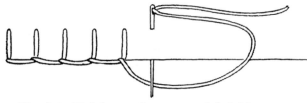

Blanket stitch is another way of finishing narrow hems or edges. It is an evenly spaced buttonhole stitch.

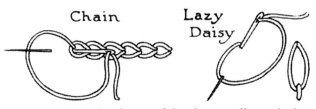

Chain stitch is done with the needle pointing toward you. Lazy-daisy stitch is a single chain stitch.

Outline stitch is a series of overlapping stitches following a line.

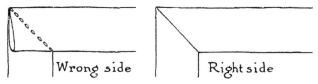

Wrong side | Right side

A miter is a little slanting fold made in a facing or band of trimming at a corner.

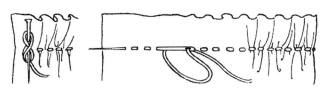

Gathers are made with running stitches. The thread is pulled up to pucker the material after the entire distance has been run. Wind the thread over a pin in a figure eight until gathers are adjusted, then rethread the needle and fasten securely.

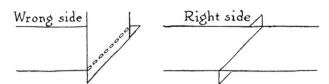

Wrong side | Right side

A joining in a bias band is always made on the straight of the material. Lap the bias edges to meet at the line of stitching.

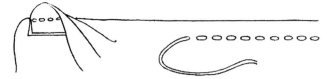

A French seam (or *pocket seam*) is sewed twice; the right side is seamed, close to the edge, then is trimmed, turned, and the wrong side stitched.

Cross-stitch is done by making two stitches of equal length crossing each other at right angles. It may be worked over canvas or directly on the material. In perfect work all the stitches of one color which slant in the same direction in a row are worked first, then the stitches slanting in the oppo-site direction are worked. This makes all the stitches cross in the same way, and it makes a neat finish on the wrong side of the material.

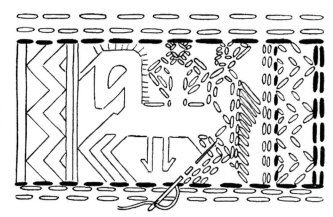

Running stitch in yarn sometimes makes a good outline for a design. Take up only a thread or two in each stitch, as in the picture.

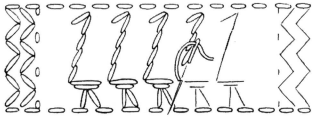

This design of ostriches is worked with straight stitches and outline stitch over an outline drawing. It makes a good band design for pockets. See how the Button-Boy bib design is transferred.

LaVergne, TN USA
28 January 2010
171473LV00001B/3/P